The Empty Nest

Finding Hope in Your
Changing Job Description

Elyse Fitzpatrick

New
Growth
Press

www.newgrowthpress.com

New Growth Press, Greensboro, NC 27404
www.newgrowthpress.com
Copyright © 2012 by Elyse Fitzpatrick.

All Scripture quotations, unless otherwise indicated, are from the *Holy Bible, English Standard Version*® (ESV®), copyright © 2000, 2001 by Crossway Bibles, a division of Good News Publishers. Used by permission. All rights reserved.

Scripture quotations marked NASB are taken from the *New American Standard Bible*, © Copyright 1960, 1962, 1963, 1968, 1971, 1972, 1973, 1975, 1977, 1995 by The Lockman Foundation. Used by permission.

Cover Design: Faceout Books, faceout.com
Typesetting: Lisa Parnell, lparnell.com

ISBN-13: 978-1-938267-80-2
ISBN-13: 978-1-938267-17-8 (eBook)

Library of Congress Cataloging-in-Publication Data
Fitzpatrick, Elyse, 1950–
  The empty nest : finding hope in your changing job description /
Elyse Fitzpatrick.
      p. cm. — (Women to women)
  Includes bibliographical references and index.
  ISBN-13: 978-1-938267-80-2 (alk. paper)
  1. Empty nesters—Religious life. 2. Mothers—Religious life. I. Title.
  BV4527.4.F58   2012
  248.8'431—dc23
                                                          2012024298
Printed in Canada

19 18 17 16 15 14 13 12   1 2 3 4 5

Not long ago, a friend and I attended Parents Orientation at our kids' college. It was an exciting time for our kids but, frankly, not for us. "How did we get here?" we both wondered. "I don't understand," my friend said through tears. "Why would God command us to pour our lives into our children and then make us let them go?" We both shook our heads in dismay.

The empty nest—that time of life when children leave home to pursue their own adult lives—can be a time of confusion, tears, and purposelessness for the parents left behind, especially the mothers. Has it been that way for you? Are you wondering, as I did, what happened to those little bare feet running through the house, to the wild screaming and laughter at swim parties, to the Little League games that seemed like they'd never end, and to the holiday dinners with everyone crammed around the table talking all at once? As a mother of three (and now grandmother to six), I know that sad and empty feeling. I remember when my youngest was married. "Okay," I wondered, "just what am I supposed to do now?"

Why *does* God give us children and then take away what he's given? As I asked myself that question, my mind traveled back to a surprising statement made by one of my college professors. He said, "Life is a series of divestitures." Over the years I've grown to see how true that statement is. Here's how the truth of lifelong divestiture, lifelong change and loss, is framed in Ecclesiastes 3:1–8:

> For everything there is a season, and a time for every matter under heaven:
>
> a time to be born, and a time to die;
> a time to plant, and a time to pluck up what is planted;
> a time to kill, and a time to heal;
> a time to break down, and a time to build up;
> a time to weep, and a time to laugh;
> a time to mourn, and a time to dance;
> a time to cast away stones, and a time to gather stones together;
> a time to embrace, and a time to refrain from embracing;
> a time to seek, and a time to lose;
> a time to keep, and a time to cast away;
> a time to tear, and a time to sew;
> a time to keep silence, and a time to speak;
> a time to love, and a time to hate;
> a time for war, and a time for peace.

Ecclesiastes tells us that life is marked by ongoing change, gaining and losing, divestiture and seasons. If this beautiful poetry teaches us anything, it is that nothing in our lives stays the same. The "time" that we're in right now, the empty nest, might seem as though it is only a time of loss. In some ways, that is true. But if you look at it from another perspective, could it be something more than loss? Could it be a time of blessing, of adding, of refocusing your remaining relationships?

Please don't misunderstand what I'm saying here. I agree that it's normal to feel loss and to grieve when there are major changes in deep and meaningful relationships. We know that grieving isn't wrong because Jesus himself grieved at the tomb of his friend Lazarus. He deeply felt the loss when his friends slept through his hour of greatest need at Gethsemane. Grief at suffering isn't sinful, but it is meant to draw us closer to the Lord who knows all about it. Grief is meant to eventually help us see that God truly understands.

We Aren't Alone in Our Grief and Loss

Hebrews 4:15 tells us that Jesus understands everything we go through.

> For we do not have a high priest who is
> unable to sympathize with our weaknesses,
> but one who *in every respect* has been tempted
> as we are, yet without sin (italics added).

Jesus sympathizes with us in our time of loss because he knows what grief and loss feel like. He knows the weaknesses we struggle with: wishing things were different, longing for the past, wanting to hear their voices around the breakfast table again. We love our children and we want to be near them—always. He understands.

It's one thing for us to assent to the truth in this passage; it's another thing to ponder it deeply. When the writer said that Jesus was tempted "in every respect" as we are, he meant that Jesus knows firsthand, by experience, what you're going through. Although he didn't have children to send off to college or give away at a wedding, he did have personal losses, as Philippians 2:5–8 makes plain.

> Have this mind among yourselves, which is
> yours in Christ Jesus, who, though he was
> in the form of God, did not count equality
> with God a thing to be grasped, but emptied
> himself, taking the form of a servant, being
> born in the likeness of men. And being
> found in human form, he humbled himself
> by becoming obedient to the point of death,
> even death on a cross.

Because his relationship with his Father changed, Jesus understands the loss we feel when our relationships change. In order to bring salvation to us, he had to take on human form. Even now he is what he never was before: the *incarnate* Son of God. He is the Son who left his celestial home to come to earth and suffer loss after loss until he ended up crying out, "My God, my God, why have you forsaken me?" (Matthew 27:46). When you feel abandoned, you can be sure that he understands it all firsthand. And God, our Heavenly Father, knows what it is like to say goodbye to a Son. The circumstances were different, but the suffering was far greater.

He's More Than Our Example

The great news about Jesus' identification with us is that he is more than someone who simply understands. He is also someone who can take what is wrong with us and make it right. In other words, he is more than our example; he is our source of *righteousness*. That is what happened when Jesus died on the cross for our sins. He took our place, paid the penalty our sins deserved, and gave us his own perfect righteousness in exchange.

What does that mean? Well, can you think of a time when you responded to the empty nest in a wrong way? For instance, have you ever been selfish, angry, full of self-pity, or manipulative? Do you know what Christ's righteousness means for you at those times? It means that in all the ways we've failed to respond to this difficulty as we should, we can know that we are nevertheless declared sinless or righteous in his sight, *if* we belong to him. That is because Jesus' suffering has brought us *justification*. This word means that if you've trusted Christ for your salvation, your record before God is "just as if you had never sinned."

That is obviously great news, but there is even more good news with justification. It also means "just as if you had always obeyed." Jesus never complained about the losses he felt. He simply kept entrusting himself to his Father. He looked forward to reuniting with his Father (John 14:28), but he was never impatient or selfishly focused on what he wanted. He never spoke evil or wondered why bad things had to happen to him. Instead, he gave himself completely to doing his Father's will (Luke 22:42). And if you're his today, this is your record too. Amazing grace!

Another reason justification is important to you today is that it takes care of any regret you may have. As a mom, I am haunted by the memory of so many lost opportunities and times when I said more than I should have and wounded my children's little hearts with my words. I remember times when I was impatient and demanding, when I tried to shame my children into obedience. Yes, regret has been my companion for years, especially since my kids moved out. There is only one truth that can comfort my heart when I struggle with regret—and it's not the truth of my record as a mom. It's the truth of *Jesus'* record. Yes, I did sin against my kids (probably more than I know), but the good news of the gospel is that God has forgiven my sin and granted to me the perfect record of his Son. God sees the righteousness of his Son instead of my sin. This is a truth I can and must believe and live out every day.

Yes, facing the empty nest is a difficult season. But we're not alone. We can get together with friends or a counselor and commiserate—sometimes that's helpful—but it's an entirely different thing to know that the Lord understands exactly what we're facing. We can go to him knowing that he hears and answers prayer.

In the School of Seasons

So let me ask this question again: why does God give to us and then take away what he's given? Could it be that he's teaching us about our nature and his? Could it be that we need to be reminded that he is to be the ultimate focus of our lives? Could it be that he wants to draw near to us through our tears?

Change and seasons have been part of our world since the first day of creation. God caused a variation between day and night and called this change "good." After the flood, the Lord promised Noah that there would be changes, but that he would sustain the earth through them all: "While the earth remains, seedtime and harvest, cold and heat, summer and winter, day and night, shall not cease" (Genesis 8:22). This promise was meant to reassure Noah (and us) that seasons would come and go, but God would maintain his creation until the end of time.

Have you ever wondered why God built change and seasons into our lives? He built these fluctuations into our lives so that we would learn about ourselves. Our need for sleep and our dependence on the rain for food teach us of our limits and weakness. We can send a man to the moon, but if the Lord doesn't send rain, we don't eat. The changing nature of our world teaches us that we aren't in charge. We can't control the seasons. We can't make rain, stop the tides, or calm the wind. We grow old, we lose vitality, and we stumble. We're dependent, needy, and weak. It is good to learn this about ourselves; otherwise we might not stop to "number our days" as Psalm 90:12 advises.

Of course, we all acknowledge that everyone is growing older and that our lives are bound to change. But when it comes to our day-to-day living, we assume that things will stay just as they are. Then the seasons change, the kids move out, and we're reminded of the truth.

The seasons also teach us about God. They teach us that he is different from us—completely self-sufficient and independent. There are no seasons for the Lord—only glorious, eternal, jubilant day. James writes that he is "the Father of lights with whom there is no variation or shadow due to change" (James 1:17). He never changes and he has assured us that we can depend on him to be "the same yesterday and today and forever" (Hebrews 13:8).

Your perspective on this season of the empty nest will be colored by what you understand about the purpose of change and what it can teach you about yourself and God and life. Your perspective on your empty nest will also be colored by the way you approach your relationships with your spouse and your kids and, most importantly, your relationship with the Lord. Let's think about that a little more.

Your Relationship with the Lord

Perhaps you're beginning to see that this time of loss might also be a time when good, new things can be added to your life. For instance, now that you're not running to soccer games or operating a taxi service for your kids, you might discover that you have more time to be quiet, to ponder the Lord's goodness in your life, to speak with him and draw nearer to him. When I entered this stage of life, I began to keep a prayer journal. I have used it to record my hopes, my desires, and, most of all, the words the Lord whispers to my heart.

As I study Scripture, I take time to record what he is teaching me and how I hope he'll work. Consequently, as my kids have left home, I've found that my relationship with the Lord has grown. I'm no longer frantically trying to fit a little prayer and Bible reading into a hectic daily schedule. I find instead that I can give blocks of time to the Lord, to the Word, to speaking with him and thinking of him. For me, that's been the most delightful part of my empty nest—finding Jesus there with me.

You might also begin to see other doors open to you. For example, perhaps you can be more involved in ministry than you have been before. Yes, you're missing your kids, but can you see how your life of nurturing others might not be over?

Frequently when God closes one door of ministry, he opens another. You enjoyed life as it was, but you might enjoy life again as you give yourself elsewhere. Perhaps you could seek out young women to mentor. You could use your desire to nurture in a Titus 2:3-5 ministry, mentoring young women who are starting their families. Many younger women today are frightened as they try to learn to be wives and mothers. Many of them lacked healthy role models or positive home experiences growing up. Could the Lord use your gifts to bless them? Mentoring younger women needn't be like formal counseling. It could be a time of getting together for coffee and offering a word of encouragement to a sister who is overwhelmed, wondering how to make it through the day. You've got years of wisdom stored up in your heart. Are you willing to share it?

Your Relationship with Your Spouse

When we think about the empty nest, we have to confront an amazing truth: you probably don't live in an *empty* nest anyway! Unless you are a single parent, you still have your husband in your home. If you have a great relationship with your spouse, you're probably looking forward to time alone with him—finally, after all these years. But if your relationship with him isn't what it once was, you might wonder how you're going to make it through the years to come. Have you considered the possibility that God has given you an empty nest to reclaim the potential of this relationship?

The truth is that our relationship with our kids was always meant to change like this—we just never thought about it until now. But the Bible is clear that our primary relationship in life is with our spouse, which is why the Bible's first command about marriage tells us to leave father and mother and build a new life together (Genesis 2:24).

We are never told to become one flesh with our children, although in one way they are part of our flesh, aren't they? But the unity of marriage in oneness and burden bearing, in companionship and intimacy, is to be shared with our spouse alone. Our children leave. "Till death do us part" is the vow husbands and wives take, not mothers and their children. God commands this transition in our relationship, and because we know he loves us, we can know that it is ultimately for our good.

The next decades of life with your husband will be shaped by what you do now. Are you willing to work as hard on your marriage as you worked on your relationship with your kids? Are you willing to rekindle the flame of love if it has dimmed? Rebuilding a relationship that has been neglected won't be easy work. Perhaps you don't even want to try at this late date. You might wonder where to find the grace to start again. Here are some ideas.

Start at the Beginning

You've probably been spending a lot of time remembering what it was like when your kids were little. Why not go back a little farther? Think back to the days when your husband was your best friend, before the kids came along. No matter how much time has elapsed since the early days of your marriage, the truth is that your husband is still your closest companion. He has been with you through it all. He knows what your life has been like, and he's probably even got some idea of what you're going through now.

Regardless of the number of years that have gone by without a meaningful conversation, you can begin again. What does your husband enjoy? What are his desires, his fears, his hopes? How does he feel about the loss of the children's presence in the home? Perhaps he's just as concerned as you are but doesn't know how to say it. Of course, he may not be where you are, but do you know this for certain? Have you sought to draw him out and understand him?

Even if you haven't had a conversation about anything except the kids for years, you don't need to despair. When you were younger you had to learn how to carry on a conversation with him. You can do so again, with the Lord's help.

Pursuing Your Husband for Christ's Sake

You can be sure that the Lord wants you to pursue your husband and seek to make your marriage strong again. Perhaps you will be successful right away; perhaps it will take time. For a while it may seem like it never gets any better. But no matter what, I can say with certainty that Jesus Christ wants you to seek to love your husband. How do I know that? Because he wants you to grow to be like him, and that's what he's done for you. He has pursued his people, his bride, through the ages. He laid his life down for you and loved you when you hated him, when you were too weak to respond to his wooing, when you were his enemy (Romans 5:6–10).

Why not begin by talking about this with your Heavenly Father? Ask him to help you walk in the footsteps of your Savior, who pursued his bride even when it meant suffering. "For to this you have been called, because Christ also suffered for you, leaving you an example, so that you might follow in his steps" (1 Peter 2:21). Maybe you feel a resistance in your heart to this. Why not ask the Lord to help you even with that? The Holy Spirit is not only a great Comforter in times of sorrow, he also knows how to give us strength and motivation to obey. He does this mysteriously, by changing our inner desires and giving us the "want to." Why not ask him for grace to say with your Savior, "Not my will, but yours, be done" (Luke 22:42)?

You can begin to rebuild your relationship by taking the first few steps toward your husband, just like you did when you were first falling in love. Cook his favorite dinner. Offer to go with him when he plays golf (you don't need to play) or watch his favorite sports team or program with him. You are not wasting time. You're rebuilding a relationship for God's glory and your good.

A Word for Single Moms

Perhaps through death or divorce you are now facing the reality of living alone as your children leave home. You may find this transition even more difficult because your children have filled some spaces a spouse would ordinarily have filled. It's so easy for that to happen. Perhaps your son was someone you relied on for certain household tasks, like repairing the car or doing the yard work. Maybe your daughter was a friend you could shop with or talk over problems with. Perhaps your love for them is more intense because you are without a husband. As a single parent, trying to regroup when your children move away can be hard if your work schedule makes it challenging to get together with friends or be involved in your church.

The apostle Paul, himself a single man, looked at singleness in a different way. He said that singleness offered an opportunity for greater service for the Lord.

> And the unmarried or betrothed woman is
> anxious about the things of the Lord, how
> to be holy in body and spirit. . . . I say this
> for your own benefit, not to lay any restraint
> upon you, but to promote good order and to
> secure your undivided devotion to the Lord.
> (1 Corinthians 7:34–35)

What would "undivided devotion" look like in your life as a single empty nester? Perhaps now is the time to renew your relationship with the Lord and deepen relationships with those in your church. It's true that you have a lot of responsibilities and this will require some extra effort, but it will be through these relationships that you find life filling up once again. Many single women find great comfort in being involved in a small group in their church. There, singles mix with families and everyone enjoys their relationships in the family of God.

Just as empty nesters who are married, you can begin your time in this season through prayer. Ask the Lord to open your eyes to women you can encourage or strengthen in their walk with the Lord. In what areas of ministry might you get involved? Are there younger single women in your congregation you might mentor? Since you both probably have to work full time, this won't mean that you have to meet every day or even every week. Perhaps you could get together every couple of weeks to pray and share what you've learned about what it's like to live without a spouse.

You could also ask the Lord to give you a connection to a godly family. Many young families don't have grandparents nearby. Could you act as a surrogate grandmother and spend a little time on weekends blessing them? All of this will require an intentional choice on your part, but the Lord is so kind in blessing our acts of faith.

Your Relationship with Your Children

Single or married, if your relationship with your kids has been good, you'll find the empty nest difficult because they brought you so much joy. If your relationship with them has not been what you had hoped it would be, you'll find this time full of regrets. Whether you miss your children or have regrets, you're probably thinking about them.

It may be that you need to communicate to your children about this new season. Perhaps you need to ask their forgiveness for past wrongs. Maybe you need to tell them that you're asking the Lord to help you make the most of the time you now have with your husband or your church family. In some cases you may need to help them be responsible adults. Although most kids are happy to leave the nest, some of them stay too attached for way too long.[1] Some of them want the independence of adulthood with all the pampering of childhood. If you are discovering that you've got kids like this, you might consider writing them a letter, expressing your love for them, your ongoing prayers, and the ways in which your relationship will now change. For instance, you might let them know that they can always come over to use the washing machine and even raid the refrigerator, but now, as adults, they are responsible for their own lives and decisions.

Smiling at the Future

Proverbs 31 describes the life of a godly woman. One of the ways she's portrayed is very helpful to those of us facing the empty nest: "Strength and dignity are her clothing, and she smiles at the future" (v. 25 NASB). "She smiles at the future." Think of that. Rather than looking at the days to come with anxiety or despair, she looks at them with a smile on her face. She's not overwhelmed with dread, but she laughs in anticipation of all the good that is yet to come her way. How is she able to do that?

Proverbs is clear that she is able to smile because she fears or reveres the Lord. Rather than fearing what might happen to her life, to her purpose for living, or to her relationships with her children, she smiles, knowing that the God she worships holds her life and all things in his loving, faithful hands. She remembers that he has been faithful to her in the past and he will be faithful to her in the future. She looks ahead to the uncertain days to come with an underlying certainty. She doesn't fear being ashamed or abandoned because she knows the One she has believed; she is convinced that he is able to care for her soul and guard what she has given to him until the end (2 Timothy 1:12).

Seasons Can Be Beautiful

What will this season be for you? Will it be a time of sorrow and grief? Yes, probably. Will it also be a season of growth and renewal of relationships? I hope so.

As I write these words, the Lord is teaching me the same thing all over again. I haven't had children at home for nearly a decade, but my husband and I have recently moved farther away from them and from our grandchildren. This move is good because I know that the Lord has arranged it, but in some ways it is difficult too. It means that I can no longer drop by for lunch or pop down to watch a few innings of Little League play. Now, more than ever, my relationship with my husband has taken center stage and my relationships with my dear children are fading in significance—just a bit.

Like you, I need to ask the Lord to grant me a heart of humility, a willingness to pray, "Not my will, but thine be done." And like you I need to trust that the Savior who knows what I'm going through will sustain me to the end. Smile at the future? Well, I'm working on it! I hope you see that you can too.

God has built ongoing change into our lives, so he teaches us to live every day in the steadfast love and new mercies he supplies for that day (Lamentations 3:22–23). Paul encourages us to forget what's behind and strain forward to what lies ahead, pressing onward "toward the goal for the prize of the upward call of God in Christ Jesus" (Philippians 3:13–14). This difficult time may be the change you need to draw closer to Christ and learn of his love for you.

The truth is that we can't go back; we can't relive the old days. Yesterday is gone. We can't make what was wrong right or even re-create the beautiful times of loving family life. Are you ready to put your past in its place, to press forward, to see God's steadfast love and new mercies? Can you smile because you know that your Savior is there waiting for you? Trust him in this new season of life, and discover all he has prepared for you.

Endnotes

1. See Elyse Fitzpatrick and Jim Newheiser, *You Never Stop Being a Parent* (Phillipsburg, N. J.: P & R Publishing, 2010).

Simple, Quick, Biblical

Advice on Complicated Counseling Issues
for Pastors, Counselors, and Individuals

MINIBOOK
CATEGORIES

- Personal Change
- Marriage & Parenting
- Medical & Psychiatric Issues

- Women's Issues
- Singles
- Military

USE YOURSELF | GIVE TO A FRIEND | DISPLAY IN YOUR CHURCH OR MINISTRY